For all the deaf children out there in this world. I hope that this little book will inspire you to be brave, fearless and to follow your dreams.

Sandra Stevenson.

The
Deaf Witch

Written by: Sandra Stevenson
Illustrated by: Gemma Montgomery

About the Author

I have worked with children for 22 years, and had many placements during that time.

The inspiration for this book came from working with deaf children at a specialist school.

I had the pleasure of working there for 3 years and was "blown away" by the dedication of the teachers and the children.

I would like to thank my colleagues and friends for giving me these memories and experience.
I will cherish them forever.

The deaf witch could not
hear at all,
Her hearing friends always
made her feel small.

She felt very sad and wanted to cry,
so she summoned her broom
and flew up to the sky.
Up among the clouds and space,
she had no problems she needed to face,

And the bright stars that twinkled
made her feel bright,
As she glided and dived through the
purple, blue night.
As the cool wind flew by her and
played with her hair,
She looked down at the world and
hadn't a care.

As the morning had broken
she glided in,
To be met by her cat,
and she gave a wide grin.

Deep in her basement
was a room full of spells,
And frozen newt eyes
and potions as well.

She worked through the night
and into the morn,

And there midst the cobwebs
a new spell was born.

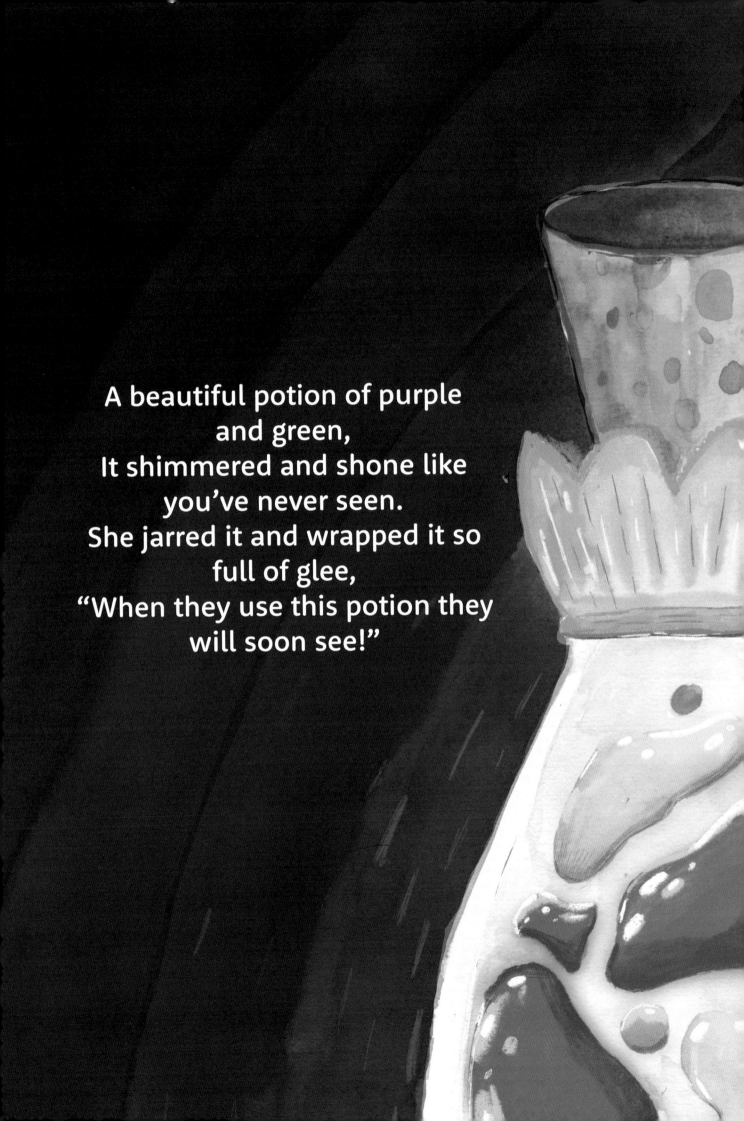

A beautiful potion of purple
and green,
It shimmered and shone like
you've never seen.
She jarred it and wrapped it so
full of glee,
"When they use this potion they
will soon see!"

And off to the market she flew
with such haste,
this surely must be the best
challenge she'd faced.

For boils,

broom burns

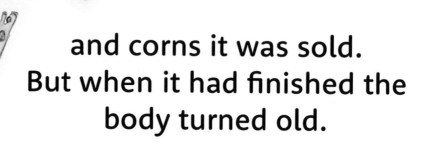

and corns it was sold.
But when it had finished the
body turned old.

And everything which had
worked perfectly before,
became rusty and old
and stiff and sore.

And the one thing which went
and never came back,
'Twas the sound in their ears,
that they soon would lack

As the people came forward
and started to buy,

The deaf witch advised them
which potions to try,

carefully keeping the best to last,
along came the witches who thought she
was daft.

"We'll try it." they said with a hint of a sneer, but next morning the after effects became clear,

and they staggered and
gasped and turned
bright blue,
as the potion rushed
through them it's work
fast to do.

As the sound in their ears became nothing at all

They couldn't communicate and began to bawl,

"its that deaf witch, she hates us."
They each tried to say, but they couldnt hear anything in all the array.

they wrote to each other

So off on their broomsticks they
flew in a group,
and rushed to her house, the
remedy to scoop.

They knocked the front door but the witch didnt hear, but she saw in her crystal ball they were near.

She laughed to herself, and patted the cat, "That will teach them" she said, putting on her black hat.

She opened the door and there stood the four, they got on their knees and started to roar.

"Please help us."
They pleaded as they held up a banner.
"That potion you gave us acted in a strange manner."

"Hello" said the witch, "we'll sort it out soon."

"But first let us go and fly to the moon."

The witches were puzzled but got
on their brooms,
and away they all flew to the
Halloween Moon.
As they glided and played they all
became friends,
and later that night the witch made
amends.

A rich golden potion made their hearing return,

And they all sat together and watched the
fire burn,

"You see", said the witch, "It isn't much fun,
When you're all left alone, and the only one."

"So remember before you discriminate,
that some day you too could inherit the same fate!

LEARN
your
ABCs

Printed in Great Britain
by Amazon